THE BLOOD BARN
is by Carrie Lorig

THE BLOODBARN is typeset in Cochin, first cut in 1912 by George Peignot, who, in 1915, enlisting after the death of his youngest brother in the Somme where over 1.5 million people lost their lives, was shot in the forehead while shouting "En avant!" / Titles are set in Harbour and Ostrich Sans.

Designed and copy-edited by 🌿
for 𝔍𝔫𝔰𝔦𝔡𝔢 𝔱𝔥𝔢 ℭ𝔞𝔰𝔱𝔩𝔢.

©Carrie Lorig, 2019

Cover photograph by Bob Lorig

A text occupying the expanded field of literature,
from 𝔍𝔫𝔰𝔦𝔡𝔢 𝔱𝔥𝔢 ℭ𝔞𝔰𝔱𝔩𝔢
www.insidethecastle.org

ITC-016
ISBN-13: 978-1-7327971-1-6
ISBN-10: 1-7327971-1-0

BLOOD BARN

Question: What happened to the lyric?

What do you think the oldest cell in your body is? It is in your brain. Do you think it is the cells that are associated with your memory / your hippocampus? I listened to men say that this is what they believed. I listened to tradition / canon say that is why we must continue to preserve and praise memory / as if it were the only thing / the oldest thing capable of song / of beauty / of meaning. The oldest cell in your body, we know thanks to all the C14 in the air from atomic atrocities in and around WWII, is mostly likely located in the cerebral cortex. It is most likely located in the part of your brain responsible for thinking / for language / for awareness / for attention / for perception. It is most likely located in the part of your brain responsible for possibility.

Question: What happened to the lyric?

Question: What happened to the lyric?

Question: What happened to the lyric?

Question: What happened to the lyric?

Question: What happened to the lyric?

Question: What happened to the lyric?

Question: What happened to the lyric?

Question: What happened to the lyric?

My body / these questions hurt

Question: What happened to the lyric?

Question: What happened to the lyric?

Question: What happened to the lyric?

Question: What happened to the lyric?

Question: What happened to the lyric?

Question: What happened to the lyric?

I'm here / I died and you can't take any more / with you I died / and there's nothing left for you to decide /

THE BLOOD BARN

I died / I'm here

I died / I'm here / Drawing / with memory / a memory a more generous kind of thinking on Drawing on / top of memory / *Do you like chocolate?* / Drawing / it bends time.

There is a certain part of my ride to wrk / every morning / I push a button for X-ing safely and often when I push the button attached to a tall pole of wood / outside of a nice house / I notice / I feel / webs touch me Always in the same place / at the intersection of Ponce and Artwood / I feel / webs reach and touch me / *Can you believe it?* / I hear a man in the story say. As I X, I pull a part of a web / velvet and sea / from my hair and walk slower / so I can look up / at light until I hear / a woman in the story say, / Your question is my project.

What happened to the lyric? / Your question is my project My body / these questions hurt.

There is a pain in my hip that I call / The Blood Barn.

This summer I was reading Edmund Berrigan's *Can It!* / quietly / When I came to / a poem called The Blood Barn / I felt an immediate / feral recognition / I felt a lost sea in / that name.

"The current Ron himself had lots of practice at killing people during his military career and was very good at it. When he entered the café, he shot his heavy drinking. He was also a list. His violent nature had led people to call him "The Blood Barn," but they never dared to name him in earshot."

This summer I was reading / quietly / when a man wrote a review of my book on Goodreads / It was a man who had tried to take something from me years ago / I told him then / No, you can't take any more / I told him then / No, you cannot contact me anymore / There's nothing left for you to decide / *Who are you / when I say / I'm afraid to let you / near me?* He was gone / until I saw this review on a website / this review[1] which bends time to hurt me / this review which tells me / which aims to disrupt me / by suggesting I am selfish because my poems write about books / quotes / citation / writing / my body / these questions hurt.

/ Is it selfish that I know how to study the present where my voice can barely exist?
/ Is it selfish that I know how to study the history

/ in which I am already an effortless / murder?

I'm not scared of history anymore /

I'm more afraid / you won't let me live now

---

[1] Which he has now deleted (Oct 30). *Because I shamed him on Twitter? Because I started filming that fucking poison without his permission?* My whole chest / breath is trembling / fire trying not to wonder if I scared him away for good or not.

/ Is it really selfish that I study / what I do? Or is it just necessary? That I care / what I do? Who are you / when you aren't with other people / when you aren't with each other? What do you do / that's necessary?

I'm not an intellectual / I'm a force I'm terrible / awe

I can't be effortless / I died / I'm here /

/ Your question is my project.

There is a pain in my hip that I call / The Blood Barn / The right side / is just scar tissue / I reach and touch it / *Can you believe it?* I feel an immediate / feral recognition / I feel a lost sea in / this space in my body / It is a swell and a poem about a secret / that gets seen and unseen again / It is a poem about the terror of imagining how much blood is in a secret It is a poem / and a secret / about how unfathomable the lastingness of suffering is It is not a secret / so much as a swell that knows / that must carry / that must hold on to how often a body is not allowed to mourn itself / in order to heal properly / I have never been armed / When I was a teenage girl / about to be 20 / I wasn't armed enough / to heal.

"The Arm was made up of men. Beta males who ate skulls decorated with beans."

The chart asks me to circle on the blue drawing of the body / where my pain is / red.

I circle the Blood Barn / I mark it thick and bright / It transmits history I am not afraid of anymore / but that I still suffer from / I am still learning to suffer from.

A lastingness that is unfathomable / *What is the secret?*
What is the poem that gets seen and unseen again? What is the terror of imagining?
Why don't I feel like I was ever allowed to feel what happened to me?
What would that even look like?

Place a mark on "Yes" or "No" to indicate if you've had any of the following:

Place a mark on "Yes" or "No" to indicate if you have had any of the following:								
AIDS/HIV	☐ Yes	☐ No	Emphysema	☐ Yes	☐ No	Migraine Headaches	☐ Ye	
Alcoholism	☐ Yes	☐ No	Epilepsy	☐ Yes	☐ No	Miscarriage	☐ Ye	
Allergy Shots	☐ Yes	☐ No	Fractures	☐ Yes	☐ No	Mononucleosis	☐ Ye	
Anemia	☐ Yes	☐ No	Glaucoma	☐ Yes	☐ No	Multiple Sclerosis	☐ Ye	
Anorexia	✗ Yes	☐ No	Goiter	☐ Yes	☐ No	Mumps	☐ Ye	
Appendicitis	☐ Yes	☐ No	Gonorrhea	☐ Yes	☐ No	Osteoporosis	☐ Ye	
Arthritis	☐ Yes	☐ No	Gout	☐ Yes	☐ No	Pacemaker	☐ Ye	
Asthma	☐ Yes	☐ No	Heart Disease	☐ Yes	☐ No	Parkinson's Disease	☐ Ye	
Bleeding Disorders	☐ Yes	☐ No	Hepatitis	☐ Yes	☐ No	Pinched Nerve	☐ Ye	
Breast Lump	☐ Yes	☐ No	Hernia	☐ Yes	☐ No	Pneumonia	☐ Ye	
Bronchitis	☐ Yes	☐ No	Herniated Disk	☐ Yes	☐ No	Polio	☐ Ye	
Bulimia	✗ Yes	☐ No	Herpes	☐ Yes	☐ No	Prostate Problem	☐ Ye	
Cancer	☐ Yes	☐ No	High Blood Pressure	☐ Yes	☐ No	Prosthesis	☐ Ye	
Cataracts	☐ Yes	☐ No	High Cholesterol	☐ Yes	☐ No	Psychiatric Care	☐ Ye	
Chemical Dependency	☐ Yes	☐ No	Kidney Disease	☐ Yes	☐ No	Rheumatoid Arthritis	☐ Ye	
Chicken Pox	☐ Yes	☐ No	Liver Disease	☐ Yes	☐ No	Rheumatic Fever	☐ Ye	
Diabetes	☐ Yes	☐ No	Measles	☐ Yes	☐ No	Scarlet Fever	☐ Ye	

I explain to the chiropractor, who has the same name as a poet, the conditions of my life when I last felt The Blood Barn / an ecstatic bruised / starvation its lastingness / a pain in my right hip.

She asks me questions that take a long time to answer.

/ ?

? /

/ ?

She touches my hip and explains that The Blood Barn / the hip / is where things are held / where things are held onto / where they reek and rot / and get rich Floral even / I tell her I've been thinking of writing this poem since I moved to Atlanta / since summer when I read Eddie's book / quietly / on our peeling / black couch.

/ I have been holding it in my body / a poem / a secret / seen and unseen again / This place where things are held / where things are held onto is the Root chakra / the mud / a circle surrounded by four lotus petals with a square inside / the red belly / the Ruby / my birthstone.

It is the chakra of the physical body / it is the chakra of self-preservation, survival, perception, fear, and safety / it is the chakra of cedarwood and sandalwood / it is the chakra of Pluto / of the sexual and adrenal glands /

of inherited trauma / My mother / my grandmother /

It is stealing to use a word like chakra / There are no words in America's wealth / for what the physical body is capable of experiencing / our banks refuse them / the words with vents / the dirt near the water / or our shame intervenes in u / until the carcass fragments and it's good and it's not The words / with vents / a sensitivity / for what the body must say.

/ Who are you

when we are not together? Who are you when we are not each other

together /

because there are no words?

What did your great beauty bring you?

/ A living
/ its skull

A beginning with nothing / A mode of beginning with nothing

THE BLOOD BARN

A picture of my root / frozen plains or fog / on Pluto

Who licks the ivy?

Dear L[2],

There are textures that sit behind the world.

Love,
C

---

[2] Leora Fridman

Dear C[3],

I am thinking of quitting poetry to sing. Maybe my voice will be more welcome there than at poetry readings.

I came here because I wanted to squeak. I came to writing in order to sing without having to train a singing voice, so that I could squeak as squeakily as I felt — I wanted to stop training toward what other people expected to see from my female body. I wanted to talk weird. I wanted to talk as weird as I talk to myself and my loved ones. I wanted my public talk and private talk to be more unified.

I have a body that fits pretty well with what people want of it most of the time. Most of the time it fits pretty well with what I want of it. I wanted to stop presenting this pretty well body in a pretty well way because I didn't feel pretty well and it felt like lying to talk pretty well.

When I give readings it's hard to figure out how to be anything more than pretty well. I'm so well trained to look pretty well and talk pretty well in public. I want to make an audience listen to something that is more than my pretty well body. Even if I wear a pretty dress to my reading. I want to make them listen to my body and more.

You wrote to me once about giving readings and how you feel your audience is always fighting you. And then, in "Reading as a Wildflower Activist / Pt. 2," you wrote:

---

[3] This letter was written by Leora Fridman and originally published on VIDA's website on September 29, 2015 with the title, "Report from the Field: Letter to C."

"A Flower is / A Fruit and A Wound,

is what I think when a Man tells me

a Man who heard me read / said,

"I wish she wrote the way she talks.[4]"

What I hear the Man say to you is: *Don't talk if I don't get it. Don't talk if I can't understand. Stop talking to me if I can't understand you. Stop talking to me in a way that confuses me. Stop talking to me in a way that makes me uncomfortable.*

I hear:

I wish she wrote the way she talks —

I wish she was just her body —

I wish she was only her body —

I wish her body was on paper —

I wish she read her body to me—

I wish she read her body for me—

I wish she read her body for me along—

---

[4] Lorig, Carrie, "Reading as a Wildflower Activist / Pt. 2", *The Pulp Vs. The Throne*, Artifice Books, 2015.

I wish her body was all there was there—

I wish she wrote the way her body—

I wish she wrote the way her body lulls me—

I wish she wrote the way she lullabies—

I wish she would lull me—

I wish she always wanted to be a mother—

I wish she played across my belly and I watched over—

I wish she played with me like a young girl should—

I always hear this. I always hear that I should play like a young girl should / that I should stop talking if that Man can't understand. That I should try to say it real pretty or stop talking.

"I wish she wrote the way she talks."

I wish I could write away from the way I talk – I wish my talking could move my body / not just my mouth. I wish my talking could move my body to a new location when often my location is stuck / feels stuck as pretty well / my body can't escape the stuckness but my speech can / my speech can fall out of the stuck.

I'm thinking now about what it means to "fall out" like in Kelin's new book (*The Gloria Stories*). Especially re: weight and women and space. It feels exciting -- a way to move beyond what now feels stale: the topic of men taking up too much space. I'm tired of talking about that, I'm tired of the tumblr of the men with their legs spread wide on the subway[5]– I'm tired of hearing myself talk about it. I GET SO TIRED OF TALKING ABOUT THAT. There's more for me than this wily wise whine –

What happens when you fall out– always? When you're always falling out of what someone else wants of you? What happens when part of your body falls away or out – or is taken out – or is told it should be taken out– what is LEFT?

Kelin on queefs: *AIR FALLING OUT IS A CONSTANT REMINDER OF THE OCCUPIERS OF SPACE.*[6]

What's left in that air? What's left in the place where the air came out of? What's in the air when our speech is there, but we are not allowed to be there? When a person writes something a man doesn't like—what's in the air?

I have to fall back on something that stays in the air. Because I'm still in the air even if no one likes what I'm saying. I want to believe there's something in the air when I read, when I write. I find myself returning to the word *soul* as a potential resource: something I never thought I would do. My father

---

[5] http://mentakingup2muchspaceonthetrain.tumblr.com/
[6] Loe, Kelin, from "Toxin Tocsin! Or the Origins of Kelin Loe!"
   http://www.spectermagazine.com/twenty-two/loe/

used to always mock spirituality but the soul has meaning to me the more I carve away / fall out–

What is left when I fall out– what is left when I fall out of talking pretty well? What is of value if no one understands me — what is of value fundamentally? When is how much space I take up relevant / irrelevant? What if nothing is of value and what, then, is that no-*thing*?

Maybe it's because I'm small– my body is small– I've always been told how small I am– cute– coming up to chest level on other people– my head is about at nipple height on my husband– cute — but I feel too large– curves etc– belly etc– I developed a butt for the first time when I was 25 and was so confused about how part of me could expand without another human inside me– I felt guilty for more air being taken by part of my body– until men started to tell me they liked it– but I still feel some of that air-taking guilt. I don't want space expanding inside me unless it can fall out.

The only way for my body to expand that is acceptable now that I am thirty: a baby — I want a baby to fall through me: not expand me, but lay upon my stomach and fall out through my back– clear out any need I could have of producing– so I don't have to talk to be honest– I only have to just produce. If I can produce I don't have to talk. My lady body doesn't need to talk to be good / pretty well– it just needs to make a baby.

What if I don't want to?

I have less money these days and I start to need — I start to buy things so I can feel good, a habit I've fallen out of for the last few years. I get anxious and I want to be more clear to people. I start to prepare again for (newly) what everyone wants from me. I fall back on talking pretty well. It is labor– emotional labor– social labor– unseen labor — but still I want to be what everyone wants from me– sometimes that's tiring but sometimes I think it's the world I want to live in.

I said to S: *I don't want to stop doing this work / I want to live in a world where everyone does this work* — I want to live in a world where everyone is doing that labor making something other people want, but/and still making themselves slippery –

Is there anything to be said that isn't what someone needs from me? This is a real question I have. This is my gender training: I'm not sure if there's anything to be said, written, or spoken if it isn't something someone needs from me.

Is there anything beyond what people need from me? What else is there? Will I ever get over who my sister needs me to be– who J needs me to be — will I ever get over who A wanted me to be / a heartache poet— a poet – so I was a poet for a man?

Did I become a poet for a man? I think in part. I came to poetry because a man let me in, and let me in again. I am ashamed to be a poet for a man — but is it possible enough time has passed so that now I am just a poet? That I am JUST as a poet / JUST in BEING a poet– as in, justice has been served and I am in balance on the scales?

The scales keep tipping– maybe that's life / what I want from life– but also always I find myself seeking what is RIGHT– Am I JUST– am I OKAY– is this labor WORTHY– does it make me GOOD –

I love (& hate) that in poetry I've come upon a labor / work / joy that will never be of value in our exchange system. In poetry school, Peter was always trying to convince us baby poets to back out while we still could. He'd say, *it will always be superfluous – that is what it IS, no one will care, no one will pay you,* and yet somehow I keep yearning, yearning to be told that doing labor as a poet is valid, valuable, good, good enough to be more than just for a man / for a person.

But what could ever be more / more worthy than to do something FOR a person? That's my bottom line question: doing FOR– I want to — to contribute, is it bad (automatically) because / when it's for a man? For a non-man person? For a group?

I pledge allegiance to speaking.

Part of the joy / job / joy of the letter / poem is to cast out to know something. To cast out — but also to fall through because to write there has to be someone there to fall through / with — I feel often I cannot write without something to fall through.

This morning I fell through Danez Smith's whole book at once / I fell through because I wanted to — I swallowed — my father used to always accuse me of swallowing books instead of reading them– he was in awe of

how fast I read but couldn't believe that I could be getting something from through them if I swallowed books so quickly.
Even in writing now, to you, I write and writing comes easily because I write FOR / TO / TO FALL THROUGH. I hope this doesn't feel like I want to fall through you– erase you– not see you— I just read in Maggie Nelson's new book about how Wayne Koestenbaum got chastised by someone he wrote love letters to, they wrote back: next time, write to me –[7]

In an interview[8] Maggie Nelson said she thinks readers should read *The Argonauts* quickly and *take it in all at once*. I want to take it in. I followed her instructions and I fell through Danez Smith's book so quickly. I thought about my own whiteness and race afterwards – consuming— did I use his book only to fall through– to charge myself up with his meaning– to make myself less guilty— to write— to write upon? I want to write with, not upon. What does that look like?

What would it be like to fall through someone / something and not take something FROM them— not take OF them? I'm so grateful that I have no penis to use as I fall through– or no penis grown onto my body– because I can't assault in that particular way. My falls don't go to that kind of assault– but where do my falls go?

I wish she wrote the way she talks–

I wish she FELL the way she TALKS–

I wish she FELT the way she TALKS–

[7] Nelson, Maggie, *The Argonauts*, Graywolf Press, 2015.
[8] "Author Maggie Nelson on fielding nosy questions about queer families: 'You have to be tough and foxy," Interview with Maggie Nelson by Chloe Caldwell, May 8, 2015, *Salon.com*

she talks and falls, writes and falls.

Does the penis always have to take something away from someone as it falls through?

Does the writing always have to take something away from someone as it falls through? The speaking?

What if taking up space didn't mean taking from?

What if space isn't finite?

Danez Smith: *I wonder what song would have to play / To make her a black blur of joy & pepper mane.*[9]

Maybe joy doesn't have to be finite. What creates joy isn't finite. But space IS finite / it is / it is right now – on this planet – in these bodies – in these races and classes we're socialized to have.

Talk of the penis filling a void that needs to be filled is over-done but: what if the void just got bigger with that filling? What if the void only just got bigger when the penis got in / near it – what if the void didn't get filled up, and always had more space left? This is not good for capitalism, to always have more space.

But also, what if you enjoy being filled up? I love to be filled up– I love to

---

[9] Smith, Danez, "Swayless," *[insert] Boy*, YesYes Books, 2014.

feel that I haven't any crannies in me that need to be filled — with books / sex / people / food— I love to *swallow* — I love to feel full— maybe because mostly other people don't force me?

But in other ways I hate to feel full / with food— it means I've not been able to control my body in the way I've wanted to— been taught to— I know pretty well how to restrict this body. I get angry, angry at myself when I am full, for letting myself get full, because it means I will get fat, have an excess / larger than the version of me I wanted: the version of me that has plenty of room to hold others / reach out to others with an offer to hold — hold anything in.

My favorite version of me is not full because it has room for anything anyone can throw at me. I will make room for it. I will find spare room for that. I will dodge to catch your needs in my spare room— are you impressed by how well I dodge and dance? Are you impressed by my room?

I make room for everyone in every place in my life except for in my writing. I don't slash out a space for everyone in my writing. This is where that Man can't find me.

Hillary Gravendyk: *pioneers slash only toward a territory / they remember*[10]

Perhaps in order to slash toward something we don't remember— something new— we can't be pioneers.

So let's not be pioneers. Let's give up on being pioneers. Let's slash away

---

[10] Gravendyk, Hillary, "Lantern Canyon," *Harm*, Omnidawn, 2012.

from what we remember. Let's not colonize new spaces. Let's not slash toward.

Perhaps in order to avoid colonizing ourselves and pioneering in this work, I cannot slash toward. I cannot slash / I must instead make room in what I have already / slash myself / let the blood be / honor this slashing behavior of making room. Let's take a look at what we have in the room.

pioneers slash only toward a territory / they remember

And also Gravendyk, who wrote this, lived with so much pain. And she made so much beauty. Maybe her saying this is itself a lesson in how we can go forward / keep in touch / slash ourselves, meaning live in the pain and slash at it rather than away from it.

Anne Carson: *Pilgrims were people who figured things out as they walked.*[11]

To walk / slash / speak.

I'm good at keeping in touch. L___ reminded me I'm so good at keeping in touch that sometimes it's hard to be my friend because no one can be as good at keeping in touch as me– she's worried about disappointing me. I reach out– I reach out– I reach out– I slash / but am I reaching up and over — am I slashing / falling out?

Perhaps I keep in touch this way because I don't want to do it in my writing. I slash out toward some pretty distant places. Can you help me

[11] Carson, Anne. "Buergette," *Plainwater*, 2000.

learn how to slash close? How to slash pretty well?

Youna Kwak on Roland Barthes: *we keep our distance from each other as a means of remaining proximate.*[12]

I'm good at keeping in touch from a distance. I like to be far– I can get filled up and still have endless amounts of room. I want to learn to slash close and survive it.

Like you wrote: *a previously closed indwelling of blood / shedding / or about to dream / Your skin scared and free.*[13]

If I keep slashing the Man at the reading might not understand me, but I might get scared and free. The Man might have to slash himself.

Brenda Hillman: *how good to be able / how good to steer & grin / thinking paraffin / & in that sentence shack / an ache of novelty.*[14]

I am able, I am pretty well, and so I must slash / I must slash at the sentence. I shack up with the sentence and then slash away. I pick a fight with it to get that ache of novelty– I say the shack is shitty and useless and back away– and then I take it back. I sing for the sentence sometimes, but only when I decide.

What I am singing for is the choice to sing an easy song sometimes, a screechy song sometimes. What I am singing for is to write a full grammatically correct sentence sometimes and sometimes not. I want us all

---

[12] http://theconversant.org/?p=7925
[13] Lorig, Carrie, "Reading as a Wildflower Activist / Pt. 2," *The Pulp vs. The Throne*, Artifice Books, 2015.
[14] lman, Brenda. "July Moon." *Practical Water*, 2011: 67.

to fall out at will. I want us all to invite ourselves to fall out only at will.

I wish I could fall out without slashing— I wish I could reach out without making anyone feel they had to– even though I want– always want–

I wish I could keep in this kind of touch.

Love,
L

Dear L,

There are textures that sit behind the world / that refuse our delusions.

I touched the ketchup bottle last night and remembered how I used to measure out exactly how many servings I had eaten. I felt how I used to write it down / how close I kept those details / how I tried to warm them.

I touched the ketchup bottle / the red ice cube between us / I felt how long it will take to write this letter to you / to push for this space

/ *Are we ever the good blood once it has melted?* Once it has melted into the earth hard / or loose around warp / the flock shadow of being / in this country I count the mud as I pack it against ❀❀❀❀❀❀❀❀❀❀❀❀❀❀❀❀❀❀❀❀❀❀❀/ as it melted against / myself To push for this space as I eat it As I eat it / do I count it Do I ask us / *Is this about loyalty or is this about the mystery between us?*

❀❀
❀❀
❀❀❀❀❀❀❀❀❀❀❀❀❀❀❀❀❀❀❀❀❀❀❀❀❀❀❀❀❀
❀❀❀❀❀❀❀❀❀❀❀❀❀❀❀❀❀❀❀❀❀❀❀❀❀❀❀❀❀❀

What do I write / to help you feel me / before I reach you? I'm not sure I'm keeping in touch But I'm reciting two (pecan) trees to you / They are married they are fucking they are talking sisters they are the Mourning Moon they are talking scar tissues in the Boiling Forest / I'm reserving space inside being next to each other /

"suffer wild animals in the company of their spinach"
-Brandon Shimoda, *Evening Oracle* (read @ lunch)

The card I picked this Halloween weekend was The Ace of Cups / *Is this about loyalty or is this about the mystery between us?* / two heavycloaked bodies in the snow

ragged lumps Their foreheads / wavering in the shape / of a pair of cupped hands / a layer of text / sliced or draped / My first thought was that it was us / My first thought was that the words were indecipherable / the layer the text in its most terrifying aspect / but the Boiling Forest / it's rotated /

❋

>>>
>>>>>>> >>>>>>>>>>>>>>>>>>>>>>>><<<<<<<<<<<<>>>>>>>>>>>>
<<<<<<<>>>>>>>>>>>>>>>>>>>
IT'S GONNA BITE YR FEELINGS OUT
>>
>>>>>> >>>>>>>>>>>>>>>>>>>>>>>>><<<<<<<<<<<<>>>>>>>>>>>>
<<<<<<<>>>>>>>>>>>>>>>>>>>

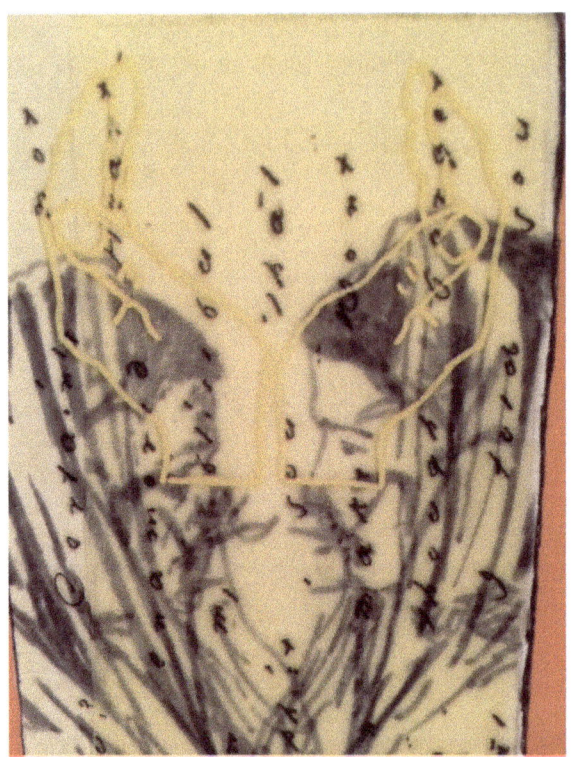

/ At a certain point the ice of one of them will have melted before the other. That person will be the good blood[15] / ❉❉

❉❉❉❉❉❉❉❉ ❉❉❉
❉

[15] Lygia Pape, Good Blood, / *do it: the compendium*

❊

Am I compelled, L, / to include this ❊❊❊❊ *from Lygia Pape's performance piece / the layer the text in its most terrifying aspect /*

because I am wishing again that I wrote poems that could be called / tenderly packed / immediately melted against a body / or listening as poems / and not these horrific details / how I tried to warm them? Is this about loyalty or is this about the mystery between us?

❊

No / I won't repeat language / this way.
❊❊
❊❊
❊❊❊❊❊❊❊❊❊❊

I remember ❊❊❊❊ sitting in the gold sequence I remember sitting in the gold roar ❊❊❊❊ of the poetry farm / our new home / while N pointed at WCW's gold piece / a wheelbarrow on the property / folded into the ghost / ❊❊❊❊ / the decay pools of pecan trees / I described to N knowing /

before I wrote poems / that I would never write poems / ❊❊❊❊❊❊❊❊❊❊❊❊❊ ❊❊❊❊❊❊❊❊❊❊❊❊❊❊❊❊ / instead I would write poems / the Boiling Forest / the layer the text in its most terrifying aspect / the mystery between us / ragged lumps of snow / sliced and draped / *Poetry, Georgia I wonder who lives there?*

❊❊
❊❊❊❊❊❊❊❊❊❊❊

Am I compelled, L, / to include this ❊❊❊❊ *because I will never be the good* ❊❊❊❊*? Is it because I will never be the good women in poetry because there still aren't any women in poetry?*

No / I won't repeat language / this way.❊❊❊❊❊❊❊❊❊❊❊❊❊❊❊❊❊❊
❊❊
❊❊❊❊❊❊❊❊❊❊❊❊❊❊❊❊❊❊❊

Lygia Pape's text insists / no one is the good ***** /

There are textures that sit behind the world / that refuse our delusions.

I will never be the good ***** I will never be the good women in poetry because there still aren't any women in poetry.

❊

(Treat me like) Treat me like
(Treat me like) Treat me like
(Fire) Fire, (Fire) Fire
(Into the pain) Into the pain
(Into the pain) Into the pain
-Lion Babe

❊

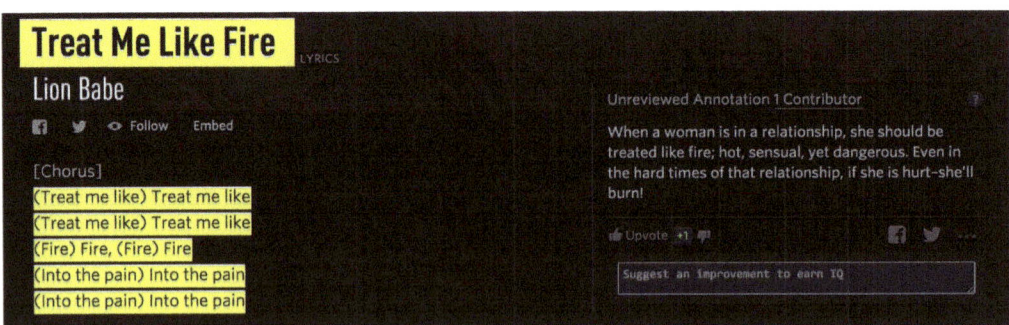

*

I went to a reading / I went to a reading in a small room / over a Jamaican restaurant / close to the rain and downtown It was painted black /

Was this the night I rode in the back of the van with large boxes? No, I wasn't reading that night. This night / I was reading / I was working. My chiropractor was there. I hugged her. I touched my hip ********** *** / the *****-soaked feathers and told her how much stronger I felt /

I asked N to help me read the parts of my poems that hold layers / another voice / the text in its most terrifying aspect. I wore a sleeve / I wore a boot / I try to consider how I can / I try to acknowledge that I want /

to express *style* sometimes / And by *style* I think I mean a seen-ness / or an encounter / an arousal or a performance of my body by my body as its only arousal / a shock I can tolerate / a shock or an opening I can offer / the *****-soaked feathers.

I got up / I said,

Who licks the ivy?
Who licks the ivy? Who licks the ivy? Who licks the ivy?
Who licks the ivy? Who licks the ivy? Who licks the ivy?
Who licks the ivy? Who licks the ivy?
Who licks the ivy? Who licks the ivy? Who licks the ivy? Who licks the ivy?

❊❊❊❊❊❊❊❊❊❊❊❊❊❊ ❊❊❊❊❊❊❊❊❊❊❊❊❊❊❊❊❊❊❊❊❊❊❊❊
❊❊❊❊❊❊❊ ❊❊❊

After the reading a woman came up to N and I /

After the reading a woman came up to N and I / We were talking / when a woman came up to us and thanked N for reading __¹⁶ poem / She thanked N for being the good ❊❊❊❊ / She called it his

❊❊
❊❊❊❊❊
          ❊❊❊
❊❊❊ ❊❊❊❊❊❊❊❊❊❊❊❊❊

I once wrote:

❊❊❊
❊❊❊❊❊
          ❊❊❊
❊❊❊ ❊❊❊❊❊❊❊❊❊❊❊❊❊

"The reading I did in graduate school / in the shadows / in the light / changed the way I thought of myself as a student / and, in turn, a reader. I was an undergraduate reading Beckett ("Then in my eyes and in my head a fine rain begins to fall, as from a rose, highly important.") for the first time in a Modern Irish and British Literature course when I called my mother and tried to explain that I realized I was very sick / anorexic. Writing with my friend E has helped me begin to understand that this expression of my

---

¹⁶ *Is it painful or is it complicated to try to place / use grammar here?* A pronoun / An article / An ownership / Grammar is always about loyalty and never about mystery.

body was very much related to my desire to be a perfect girlstudent / to prove I was not a guest / a thief / to prove I was intelligent / that I would do anything to feel alive in language / despite the fact that my sentences were too poetic / observant but unpredictable / in the ways they fleshed themselves out. The result of shaking. The result of trembling / before. How can I be real, How can I speak, I asked myself to the point that my body touched its own explosion and bled. In graduate school, I realized I could no longer / disappear."[17]

I once wrote:

                      I could no longer / disappear

But I still do /

But I still / won't

❈❈

I saw A for the first time since our tour / In Support of Repulsive Women / in Ohio last weekend. *What does the body that manifests / the stone that manifests / know in advance?* We surprised her and J. A's hair and sweater is beautiful / is the reason all the questions in this poem are italicized / "Eleven thousand times, I am a stranger / Passing artifacts, ruins, afflictions, the path / Parting

---

[17] "The Intensity of the Reader: Reading as a Guest / as a Thief in the Classroom / in the Wreckage", VIDA, June 29, 2015

from the heart, maybe / I am a girl after all the girls, I said, I mean / That is what I told her" –Brandon Shimoda (read on the bus / a few stops from the poetry farm). She / in hair and margarita / so beautiful / hands me a stone wrapped in brown paper. *How do we carry all that happens to / __*[18]*? I want to help U feel U / I want to be with U when I'm not / How should I?* "The horror of abstraction," N says on the bus / with me. The stone is chunky and the color of this poem. It was made by burning / an amethyst / the Boiling Forest in the cupped hands against your forehead. It is powered by the Sun / you hold it to your Solar Plexus / and it becomes the stone that manifests / the physical healer / the active healer / the Merchant's Stone / the stone of sex + $ in the hands of a woman / Is this the world / that manifests Does it know in advance / We called her Jewels stuck to the mountain the bodies stuck / to the rock to the sea /

astonished at the brokenness we felt I experience / everything / in my body I'm not sure you can imagine how much it is told to hold how it must rash and peel and swell to hold more / a poem a secret seen and unseen again / This place where things are held Is this the world / that manifests / I don't trust decorating / the language, the details, the abstraction that folds / her Jewels stuck to the mountain / the bodies stuffed there / The horror of abstraction, N says on the bus / with me. He says it about a student who didn't read the book / but tried to speak about it as though he had / as though he could fathom what was not only unfathomable / but had been ignored by choice / his choice / I know anything could've happened / my consumptive son / but what if what happened is he didn't have to listen when he was asked to hold it / to hold it in his body / but what if what happened is he could say something vague until the details didn't matter

---

[18] *Is it painful or is it complicated to try to place / use grammar here*? A pronoun / An article / An ownership / Grammar is always about loyalty and never about mystery.

The horror of abstraction I hope this haunts you, N said in reply / I hope this book haunts you

❀❀
❀❀
❀❀
❀❀❀❀❀❀❀❀❀❀❀❀❀❀❀❀❀❀❀❀❀❀❀❀❀❀❀❀❀❀❀❀❀❀❀❀❀❀❀

There is ❀❀❀❀ everywhere
There / ❀❀❀❀ everywhere

❀❀❀
❀❀❀
❀❀❀
❀❀
❀❀❀
❀❀❀

<<<<<<>>>>When A hands me the stone wrapped / in brown paper / I feel intensely / that A sees me / a lavender smudge in the Boiling Forest How our bodies survive How

our bodies find themselves / thriving there harshly / refusing a word like survive[19] / I know because the life of a stone / emphasizes the heavy soreness of the body stuck to the rock about to burst / stuck to the mountain lifting / the physicality of healing / the stone that manifests / my body has spent much of its life manifesting / space / a thrilling witness / in language where there isn't any space in language / a thrilling witness to the danger where there is space in language / in the world / for the stuck body / for what is about to burst / Yr poems r so intense / They're so intense! / Yr poems r so intense!!! /

I went to Ohio last weekend and M asked me a /?/ as I sat in front of his students / holding the stone A gave me with her hands / roses held above a turquoise strain of water / a turquoise strain of rock / something shredded throughout / w/ ribbons. I answered. I said, My body tries to save me vividly / It swells My eyes / they swell when I'm in danger / They flake a little My fingers peel or I rash when I'm in danger / My breath gets a rash and it swells and my breath explodes / is sometimes a scar / The Blood Barn / I hold in my hip / It has always been painful / to be saved by my body / It has always been intimate /

The first time my body / the physical alarm / the physical healer went off inside the language inside a dirtywindow / of classroom / I almost died / I almost disappeared / Because I couldn't eat / I couldn't see myself mouth /

---

[19] Survive-or / Live or Die / Vive or Die / Live w/ our terms of your survival our distrust of you / your dent our less of / you or die / Walking with (another) A, a painter / performance artist, after lunch at the School of Public Health, I tell her the flares of pain my body has been in / during the writing of this poem / The Blood Barn, it's travelled / hasn't it, says my chiropractor / pressing higher up on my back / A and I talk about not being able to get up / I describe how deeply I've been thinking of this word survive-or / how I've been trying to break it / to pull it open / "What if I'm not interested in these choices I've been given / choices I'm supposed to be grateful for," I tell her / and she stops and whips around in the wind and I feel how much she sees me / tho we've only just met and we swoon / they are talking sisters they are the Mourning Moon they are talking scar tissues in the Boiling Forest / I'm reserving space inside being next to each other /

The BLOOD BARN / Carrie LORIG

in the world / in the world that doesn't want so many of us unless we're in moneyed suffering / moneyed happiness A living backslash / who smiled up at the flannel person she was having sex with when he made fun of how much she was eating / for the first time in three days / Yr gonna get fat! Yr poems r so fat!! They're so fat!!

When I was a teenage girl / about to be 20 I entered a wordless state / It is still painful and intimate / still wordless though No, I won't survive this way No, I won't repeat language this way / because I do intend to word it To arm her / I came to poetry to speak / A stabbing unfolds I wait for it and I look it /

> I was reading. I recognized myself in the histories of sexual trauma -- a wrecked erotics that Winton tracks. I recognized my relationship to narrative -- especially as it happens or has begun to happen in Ban and Schizophrene -- reversed here -- in the language of Winton. The three markers of trauma and narrative, from a clinical point of view, are these (the first two I feel like we know, but the third one came as a shock):
>
> 1. A "wordless state."
>
> 2. A wordless state, that is, that unfolds in a "timeless way."
>
> 3. But also: "without a context."
>
> Is it that the context is "persistently disorganized"? No, it's that the context is not there.
>
> A WORDLESS, TIMELESS NARRATIVE WITHOUT A CONTEXT.
>
> THERE IS NO CONTEXT.
>
> What does Winton mean? Am I reading him correctly? The context: is not there. Because this, readers, resembles -- in its entirety -- the way I would describe -- the attempt -- to remember landscape and touch -- that happened -- in a place -- so far away -- that there is no point in returning to it. It no longer exists. It is gone. It has been, to use the emotional language of these notes: destroyed.

Bhanu Kapil's Blog, December 8th, 2015

My chiropractor touches my back with just the tips of her fingers / as part of a healing exercise / and my whole body shivers and she says my body and I / we are very close / I went to Ohio and I answered a / ? / by saying that I can only insist that my body is real / that we are very close /

*

Question: What is it like for you to communicate? / What do you want to communicate?

To listen to / or describe a difference in thinking
To receive / transmit a difference in thinking
The first time N described the way he experienced thought /
I felt terrified /
Part of me wanted to leave /
F told me / the way I described
/ thinking / feeling / while we were
living together / made her wonder
if / she was a dead person

M asked me this question and I held my stone and I tried to say how writing remains / an unimaginable activity / Love Fell / it landed so private so disgusting / that it shouldn't exist / that it is carnage / to listen to it for long /

To pack against To melt against yourself:
The ability to insist on being close

to the unspeakable revolution / of thought's texture
/ someone else's We read in a wreckage

It is an incredible boundary / A king so far from a king / that is somehow open / alive / malleable / *Who are you when I'm not with you? Who are you when I'm not with you / but we are together?* Distance is contorted or it contains a rhythm Their thoughts / migrate / egg stars in the vein a public howling / the thinking of others / streams through the world sliced and draped We read in a wreckage / what does touch and why Can I spend my life how / do I ask you what you think Can I spend my life how / do I keep giving up loyalty for mystery / for what is between us / all around me are beings

Dear L,
There are textures that sit behind the world
/ that refuse our delusions.

My experience of the world / the motion of it has always been / the sudden color of this poem / the stone in my hands / a sharpness so soft it is carnage / The Boiling Forest / her Jewels stuck to the mountain I must speak it until I am her / The Woman Ironing, I am her / or longing My body taught me poetry / it asked me about impact / in order to save me / vividly It is turbulent / immense There is nothing I can do with your comfort / the decoration of language the horror of abstraction / I have nothing to do with clarity / Instead of surviving what I do / is not hide / That's what they mean when they call me / aggressive / I just walked outside in my black boots and asked her to marry me / the ***** soaked feathers / the secret / the poem seen and unseen again If I marry her / If I am her / I am not bound to her

/ but am part of her boundary / what courses through her reach I weep it I hold it / everything to do with what is breaking /

*

A girl / a student / who heard the question M asked me / the answer I tried to say / A girl / a student who didn't see / ? / what I was holding in my hand / the stone while I spoke A girl / a student / writes to me / She says, OBJECT TRANSFORMATION.

There is a soft green stone.
There is a stone made out of snow.
There is a stone orienting to the sharp sound / of pins.
There is a black stone with small bowls for air.
There is a stone coated in thread / made of wood.
There is a stone / her palm / a little rice cake.
There is a stone painted gold.

Bhanu Kapil's Blog, December 10th, 2015 (quote / dandelions: Christina Peri Rossi's *State of Exile*) + Audrey Patts (M's student at the Art Academy of Cincinnati)

❊

A girl / a student about to be 20 / writes to me and says,
in the dark / the record.

A girl / a student about to be 20 / writes to me and says,
I found color.

❊

I am wordless here

❊

\>>>
\>>>>>>>>>>>>>>>>>>>>>>>><<<<<<<<<<<<>>>>>>>>>>>
<<<<<<<<>>>>>>>>>>>>>>>>>>>
I COULD LEAVE THE PARTY WITHOUT EVER LETTING U KNOW
\>>
\>>>>>>> >>>>>>>>>>>>>>>>>>>>>>>><<<<<<<<<<<>>>>>>>>>>>>
<<<<<<<<>>>>>>>>>>>>>>>>>>>

❊

> **Leora Fridman**
>
> I'm just eager
>
> *Yesterday 11:48 AM*
>
> Happy new year, dear C. What a blessing to live with your work / words this year. May 2016 bring molten blossoms.

*

Dear L,

This morning I rubbed vetiver / nutmeg / cinnamon / ginger / myrrh / into the stone of my palm / I smeared the smell of ***** / wet stone that comes from my root / and I felt how long it will take / it has taken to write this to you / to push for this space / that is still / only emerging / and so painfully

I'm sore and feel endlessly stupid / trying to word something like this / what happened when I was a teenage girl / about to be 20. A teenage girl / about to be 20 / who two years later moved to the mountains to save herself from trying to kill herself via refusing to eat via expelling / what icing what education she consumed / because she'd rather kill herself than listen to what was appropriate about a death / a wound / her mouth / a choice that was made for her / and what she did out of desperation to / end it / to disappear from it.

I remember my first evening facing the mountain / the sun against it / I sat on the dryer / counting the hidden honeyhives on the slope / smoked / and was sure I wouldn't / make it / because / *why would I?*

The dark did record / it as that. A girl who understood that she felt she had to become nothing. Not out of vanity / but out of a search for expansion / words in The Boiling Forest / decimation. I don't / glamorize / I don't rank this death I felt dying its impact on my body / a color I found that turned to poetry I have feeling / which is also illness / that continues and was altered against mountains.

(sent to L)

I will never write poems that look like poems No, I won't repeat language this way On the bus with N / the Woman Ironing / my husband my wife my boundary / I say, Writing today / Writing I feel I am nothing like / Alice *why would I / be* There is no music in me / just details / how I tried to warm them / A barrenness An encounter

Residual grief A body / resided in notes Notes / resided in find love where? I'm writing / a poem about a fucking rock, I say to N / It's not the first time / a texture

the song brutal or delicate / He reminds me who buried hers in Iowa / Break the song / is what she says / though I remember it as / Break the song into the song / and have been thinking on that / "call me anytime because my pain goes wet," says my playlist / The Blood Barn / the one with the violets in her lap / goes astray /

We end the year or a night listening / to music from an abandoned house / the dark does record / I make a GIF of S + S dancing blue and magenta / N standing on the couch brushing his fingers on the ceiling / My husband via Judge Ca$H the Woman Ironing / the one with the violets on her lap / goes astray / His breath turns /

His breath turns to mine when mine / gets a rash and it swells / my breath explodes / is sometimes a scar / expelling too much refusing too much / sliced or draped I feel sore today / my whole back and arms Gnarled Limbs from / heaving panic holding it out to U / while we watched a TV show called *Rectify* Each / pecan tree has its own skeleton I remember / calling J once in the middle of an anxiety attack and explaining that I was sure / I must have absorbed something I must have opened and caught / something

My body has its own skeleton / ? / that made me feel this way / so delirious / spinning / hovering above the ground while also being crushed by it / A little bit of ***** flaking or a stone / dying

What is a jewel, R asked me / Fucked up rocks gone floral, I answered We laughed in the little message box / the little message box My body and I / we are very close / My poems and I / we are very close / Language and I / we are not very close *why would I / be*

To listen to / or describe A difference in thinking / *Who are we when we are not each other together / because there are no words* / I call N and ask him to marry me or I tell him about the woman who stopped me / at work / to talk about how she keeps finding evidence / students who throw up in the bathroom / boys and girls /

I want to describe a difference in thinking / that I have no language for / We delicately train / for no language Our difference A mystery Our loyalty An ignorance / We have no language / just an arrogant / matter[20]

The folding ocean / A starving girl Scar tissue / woke up in the middle of the night because the ice cracked and it shook the lake and it shook the abandoned house / All around me are beings At a certain point the ice of one of them will have melted before the other

/ That person will receive / transmit a difference in thinking / ***** An offering / The first time N described the way he experienced thought / I felt terrified / Part of me wanted to leave / The Blood Barn A starving girl The

---

[20] But the dark / it does record. "I told you I am the night. But no one among you bothered to know what that means." -"/ *premonition*," Etel Adnan

folding ocean / I am her / I walk / beside her / How we collect it / the form one long blackened / one stone what courses through her reach / the body's edge / is lit How it waits for us / I once wrote / *How do you envision the poem beginning, L?* / and now a more feral proposition: / to recognize each other in huge water / in ✽✽✽✽✽.

I love you.

C

It is hard for me to write after it

city of tingling spring / coil The universe
city of tingling spring / coil The universe
city of tingling spring / coil The universe

city of tingling spring / coil The universe

The left side of the face /
emotes slightly stronger
than the right A mien to
move a Queen (Emily
Dickinson) /

Blood A Darkness My root My mother in January / in Chicago looking to the left

I woke up in January /

I woke up in January Fukked / on NyQuil Charcoal glitter / in the water Charcoal glitter in the throat / A mien to move a queen (Emily Dickinson) / Proteins

        of living things R left handed Meteorite / fragments that fall across the frozen surface show left handed excess / Charcoal

glitter in the water Charcoal glitter in the throat / Proteins of living things Fragments that fall across / my mouth show left handed excess Blood A Lake

        Turned Dark against / Discarding against the side of my Drinking Place / my mouth is Somehow A Lake Turned Dark

Somehow life is choosing a shape Its mirror image can be incredibly / poisonous A morning sickness / It's 3 AM and I've woken up in January to pee but there's

        so much Blood on the left side of my face I hold up my phone / pull back my lip to talk To call N in To talk a picture

Leaves burst forth in growth To talk a picture of what's happening

city of tingling spring / coil The universe Two brown holes
broken on the inside / of my Drinking Place The queen
of wands is described

as looking / out and away 2 her left / as if observing
something of interest /

It is hard to write after it To write after The Blood Barn / to write after The Blood Barn for L / Somehow life is choosing a shape Somehow a part of it / is poisonous and mine I wake up with it in my Drinking Place I wake up with it / To wake up while it's still dark / To wake up with gratitude To wake up preferring to know this is indestructible This feeling that is also illness / is not supposed to last / beyond the appearance of it / ?? / The weak little body / ?? / *How do you choose your form* / ?? / This is indestructible The weak little body The Blood Barn / She never felt like ruin to me I never felt ruined An exploration of Stein saying, "Anything shut in with you can sing" I never feel ruined though it is poisonous and mine My life it comes and goes It comes and goes The work of allowing grief I still feel / the work of allowing grief I never felt ruined That girl was waiting / She was Suspended / All the pollen is about to drop to cover says the young blond student I'm so fucking tired of the narrative that EDs are nothing but abject misery when the social rewards of thinness are so fucking profound says the young blond writer *But is that what I did it for Was I paid enough for it / Was I paid enough for how it continues / ?? /* For how it is indestructible beyond the appearance of it / The women that lived with The weak little body / don't speak to me The doctor told me to try Eating / butter My mother suffered / the love in my life My life it comes and goes It comes and goes To the love inside my life / I was a stranger and that is why I write after it That girl was waiting / She was suspended *Can you describe her choice How much / she seems to be enjoying it* I don't disagree but I will insist that I wanted to end it Anyone's ability to see or be near my body / I didn't want a fucking body / I wanted thought Hard salty soil Bursting open / one Changing Line / It was selfish and painful It is hard to write after it The question I should ask is *What does this poem need? What can I give this poem* Instead I ask if I will ever finish it This poem / The answer I get is Family member: Eldest Daughter Body Part: Thigh Season: Early Summer Image: Wind, Wood / Close to the Grain, Broad Forehead, Threefold Return The answer I get is, "This ruin wasn't caused by evil, but by indifference to decay" *And isn't that what*

I am Unable / to be / indifferent to her decay How it comes and goes It comes and goes Below the answer an egg is whipped in a steel bowl Another open tab says there is no wrong way to process trauma but there is a better way for women to take down the famous men who hurt them I don't give a shit / what happens to famous men You are a transgression that I know / has occurred Family Member: Youngest Son Body Part: Hand Season: Late Winter Image: Mountain / Watchman, Fingers, Rat or Gnarled Tree *Are the women seeking revenge* "Study their journals, watch for markings that dare to map" *or have they chosen to speak / Do they save what you have abandoned Who is beyond repair* The lining of the universe A beam touches her spine The weak little body / *Is it a girl who is unable to be indifferent to her decay* / city of tingling I wake up with it in my Drinking Place I wake up with it To wake up while it's still dark / To wake up with gratitude To wake up preferring to know this is indestructible This is only / immediate / This is only Bloodthirsty sap / "Just by addressing yourself / the problem you exhibit After crossing, devote You exhibit Whispering / Pebbles / How these things help / Poetry and Rage / one Changing line After crossing, devote" I've never been a famous men I've never been a "gift to us all" / I'm just a bitch w/ hips so tight they turn down and 2 the left in excess / or a recording that won't ever convince you of how much she can describe To the love inside my life She is not a stranger and that is why I write after it The Blood Barn that is why I will never finish it / my life it comes and goes It comes and goes

Surprising Carnations + Fish = Book
Surprising Carnations + Fish = Book
Surprising Carnations + Fish = Book
Surprising Carnations + Fish = Book
I heard a book a sea hallucinate, I heard suns plosive

plums love with fruit like falls, I heard the fish give

mass devour the rose fleshes of carnations without

protections
Surprising Carnations + Fish = Book

THE BLOOD BARN

"take shelter from the reverence which covers all women"
(*To the Lighthouse,* Virginia Woolf)

✺✺

She asks me questions that take a long time to answer.

/ ?

? /

/ ?

✺✺

My beautiful friend J My beautiful body was here
My beautiful friend / My beautiful body

We sat on the back porch and looked out at the poetry farm The pecan trees are so new they are lime / green Who can bear it /

We talk about how it felt to wake up /
with blood coming out of the left side of my face
/ We laugh / about me screaming
/ about me being so filled with /
the changing earth / a dream to know /
that I had / opened myself / Stupidly or
/ Extravagantly

When we stop laughing J / my beautiful friend / says, *What are you / writing? What are we / writing?* It's important / the questions put tenderly / and suddenly towards / the flayed flower *What kind of space does it take?* / says B in a letter / *Are you still / where you were living?* / says B in a letter *Is the erratic punctuation missing or is it intentional* / says the editor to the blood coming out of the left said of my face *Is it easy to forget* The word is a hard look that may go on[21] would have been the thing to say / to reply with / to move a hurt cardinal out of the road when before / you didn't / The word is a hard look that may go on / would have been the thing to say / but instead I said / I'm writing The Blood Barn

/ I'm writing / about my eating disorder / The one I had or have / To move a hurt cardinal out of the road when before / you didn't / The one I have

---

[21] Reading @ desk: "Language is Migrant" by Cecelia Vicuna @ Harriet on April 21, 2016.

The BLOOD BARN / Carrie LORIG

Eating disorder is a phrase / and not a word / it's a phrase that doesn't go on / I have a destiny / my death did not complete it / it makes SENTENCES These This couldn't understand how they came to be born An essay about distance and estrangement / An essay about learning how to speak / *What is a descendant of sensitivity*

❋❋❋

"If we're going to heal / let it be glorious"

"If we're going to heal / let it be glorious"

"If we're going to heal / let it be glorious"

❋❋❋

"1,000 girls raise their arms"

"1,000 girls raise their arms"

"1,000 girls raise their arms"

❋❋❋

My dress came in the mail and it's cardinal and orange and burnt and brick and it's maybe a little big and pulling away from my body My death did not complete it / J + I are driving to the bar to celebrate / after his reading / when I shout, Surprising Carnations + Fish = Book / We are laughing J + I We were sitting on the back porch and looking out at the poetry farm / "Yes, I deserve a spring—I owe nobody nothing" / the early sunflowers / when I said, I'm writing The Blood Barn / I'm writing / about my eating disorder / The one I had or have / We are laughing and then we're not because Eating disorder is a phrase / and not a word / it's a phrase that doesn't go on / How to explain that I am going to allow it to go on / How to explain that it may That it is almost May and I contain it / as a hard look that does go on *Are you still / where you were living? What kind of space does it take?*

❊❊

I have / haven't met B in person. One time in Boston… / *What happened?* I remember I spoke to B about the same things I do now *What is a descendant of sensitivity* /

Do you live in a state of repercussion says B and I resist /

I tell N in the yard / in the early sunflowers / I was going to say No to B's question, but know it is / a question I need / It takes a long time / to answer / To answer I describe the first time I saw a tank in the mountains / how I laid down in a ditch with my bike / To answer I describe a tank in the mountains / how it ground over the concrete *Is this how / I live* / I wanted to say No / because the word repercussion It is a surprising word to be asked about The roses / devour the flesh The rose fleshes of carnations Alien blue / light in the devour / The word Absorb has suddenly / become impossible says N in the early sunflowers / It makes me feel / I'm only a reaction / a state of recoiling / a state of retching / *What is a consequence Who is a consequence* How does she live But Repercussion is a word / I need I need / a question about the stretch between I need a question put tenderly and suddenly towards The stretch between organized throbbing and what can fray / The red silk falls to the ground and nothing grounds over it / it converts it There is a commute

What is a consequence Who is a consequence I'm ashamed of what I can imagine and what I cannot / A starving girl must say Yes to Repercussion / because I don't think giving word and feeling to the starving girl / to the bleeding body I don't think a hard look that may go on is about resistance / A cut is not untouched A cut proliferates distorts proliferation / I don't think her refusal / was or is about leaving any part of the world This is what memory really is / my loved men bodies She ground over it / Repercussion / A complicated integration in the early sunflowers / The starving girl She asks not to be momentary She asks to speak / The starving girl / She said Yes / She says Yes so she or the world could / see could listen to / all the room in B's questions I am reactive I am flinching or free There is the phrase that doesn't go on but then there is the surprising word and the girl Flesh of carnation Who folded in on herself so that her thinking / her pain could be exactly as private as it was public / *What is a consequence Who is a consequence*

The BLOOD BARN / Carrie LORIG

I didn't have a regular period A form of oil in their bodies until I was 25 And even then…*What happened*? *What happens to me?* This writing is private It's Overgrown It's an invitation / to read what can't be read What I can't write The Blood Barn It is hard to write after it To write after What couldn't have happened but does happen A form of oil The Blood Barn is their bodies The Inexpressible / Red Garnet Menstruation Ketchup Ember We have sex and / joke about it hitting the sides / of my Ketchup / bottle hitting the sides of My desire to kill / U hitting the sides of My desire to kill / the reverence which covers all women / "You look nice with your hair down" "Your shoulders look burnt" "Did you hurt your wrist hitting men?" "I wish" How is a citation, something you've never read, a thing you are reading This writing / is private This writing / is public It is a cave It is a petty grove / IT IS A WISH The Inexpressible / A Red Gladiolus / *Is it a* PEEL / *? Doesn't it* PEEL / *?* A note a long pause Length: It is color but it is also fur Unravelling and arranged It needed a fire to release

❊❊❊

the girl Flesh of carnation Who folded in on herself so that her thinking / her pain could be exactly as private as it was public

She asks me questions that take a long time to answer.

/ ?

? /

/ ?

❊❊❊

What is anorexia to the girl?

✽✽✽

How did you emerge?

How did you live?

How do you continue?

Who are you when we are not each other together?

Who alive would

Who alive would

Who alive would

Who alive does mind her?

✽✽✽

I touched the ketchup bottle last night and remembered how I used to measure out exactly how many servings I had eaten. I felt how I used to write it down / how close I kept those details / how I tried to warm them.

I touched the ketchup bottle / the red ice cube between us / I felt how long it will take to write this to myself / to push for this space.

❊❊❊

What turns the phrase that doesn't go on? What softens it? I had a small amount of time left in England. I had been in the library for months. I had barely spoken to anyone for months. Everyday I showed the guard my empty pockets. Everyday I could only take pencils into the archive. I had a small amount of time left in England. A photo in the wind. A photo at Stonehenge shows excess / in my jeans / in the wind. I remember buying pumpkin seeds, barfi / a forest green diamond in East London. I remember buying a tent from a French girl. I remember buying a backpack from a French girl. The last of the money went / to a French girl and a bus. L agreed to go with me to Scotland, agreed to walk 96 miles with me. The West Highland Way. We left excess, clothes and a suitcase, at a nightclub in North London. L had made friends with a singer who was born at a truck stop. He sang and gave us space for excess. A photo of me washing my clothes in a bathtub. A little bit of blood on a shirt. The excess in L's boots / made her walk bleed. Taking the route in this direction keeps the sun from a body's eyes. N texts me this morning, "I hope there will be a whole series of books by women all called *The Hermit* that aren't explicitly linked," and I think, putting my hand or / the center of a flower / on pain, "That is what it feels like to write this." I also think, "That is the title of the body." *The Hermit* / *The Blood Barn* / the poem that gets seen and unseen again A swell A body not explicitly linked. The food stuck in its throat. We walked and I felt relief. It wasn't numbness / I felt nothing / but shape, the life of it. I ate but I had an explicit need / direction / an explicit movement across the silent comfort of difficult land, difficult animal. Cereal and peanut butter for the first time in months or years. Sleep on the ground and in the middle of sheep or cows. A boat in black water. A calmness about it, an envelopment. A night so cold we slept in the showers / of a campground. Red sky at night, sailor's delight Red sky in the morning, sailor's take warning, said the young man who handed us each a tall beer. I have always been disciplined. I have always been able to push the body that is also The Boiling Forest / my mind. I cut my hair so I could walk back and forth. I cut into my body so I could walk back and forth. I never thought I would write about this, about making this decision to walk and to cut. The great broken heart tucked in that was also not broken, but Blank and also opening. *What turns the phrase that doesn't go on? What softens it?* Bones and blood erupt *How is the memory of / an eating disorder also part of / the red gate lurching.* The girl faces freedom and it is excruciating. Are shitting flowers / Is a phrase / Is a word that goes on / a typical intervention. Do they take us out or do they take us out. I cut my hair so I could walk back and forth. I cut into my body so I could walk back and forth. I walked to the edge of the mountain and went forward. I stood at the top of a mountain called Ben Nevis with the Germans I'd met. I stood at the top and thought about what is both black and green about the mountain, a mountain or the shining body / of a thing that flies. They asked me what it felt like to come all this way without boots.

❁❁

I put the food in the garbage and put dish soap on top it.

I put the food down the shower drain.

❁❁

What stops / an Earth a Cosmos the terrestrial drama / of remembrance /

a body of little suns I cut a body into little suns / a body of little suns I cut a body into little suns / a body of little suns I cut a body into little suns // a body of little suns I cut a body into little suns / a body of little suns I cut a body into little suns / a body of little suns I cut a body into little suns / a body of little suns I cut a body into little suns / a body of little suns I cut a body into little suns / a body of little suns I cut a body into little suns / a body of little suns I cut a body into little suns / a body of little suns I cut a body into little suns / a body of little suns I cut a body into little suns / a body of little suns I cut a body into little suns / a body of little suns I cut

The BLOOD BARN / Carrie LORIG

I would say The secrets of great combustions / seen and unseen again *Who are you /*

when I say / I'm afraid to hear myself talking about singing myself?

Who was I / when we were not / each other together?

A non-living World / or a ceremony I would say I did live as a ceremony / a sequence with Raw Mango /

❋

I would say I want to give you / what I remember,
I would say that I remember what happened

/ that I don't

/ *do I translate*
"so does my body"

❋

I remember calling my mother / Unable / to remember how

/ to eat the food,
/ a Raw Mango

/ a little sun

                                        I cried holding / the food I couldn't feel
                                        A fruit / I couldn't eat / on the couch
                                        I stunned myself / I didn't realize how
                                        successful I'd become /

I made myself so able to forget
/ I had made myself

few women ever experience themselves as real
few women ever experience themselves as real
few women ever experience themselves as real
few women ever experience themselves as real
few women ever experience themselves as real

❋

I thought this would be like an essay
but in my life / I've never written prose

❋

                                    I don't mostly cry
                                    and so pay for having been
                                    myself A girl A bruised
                                    ecstatic starvation Mostly
                                    as a dream hole I feel I lived

other kindness dangerously another / A woman She could be unreal /

                                                crumpled Tulip
Mostly I lift my shirt and look at
                                                a workshop on revenge,
                                                the lyric, ekphrasis,
                                                my first class on literary theory,

a workshop on obsessing the line As unreal /
crumpled Tulip, a workshop on being tangled
up, over thrown, more volatile and

                                                        trailing / rose-like
                    clusters

*

It's summer and everyone is writing
on a small paper The Truth the Dead Know

It is June. I am tired of being brave. I lift

my shirt and only ever see

                                                     a workshop / the body / cut into
little suns nobody asks a question about it / the body could forget
      how to eat / It could not forget the word is a hard look
           that may go on / and so,

                                        hunger stayed / a small century
                                 / a ceremony inexpressible / or skinning

            me alive in a garden

"Yes, I deserve a spring—I owe nobody nothing"

                                        "so does my body"

❊

            I'm ashamed of what I can imagine and what I cannot /
A starving girl must say Yes to Repercussion / because I don't think giving word
    and feeling to the starving girl / I don't think a hard look that may go on
is about resistance / A cut is not untouched / I don't think her refusal / was or is
about leaving any part of the world This is what memory really is / my loved
        bodies She ground over it / I am deliberately watching
              the transcriptions from inside me /

❊

I am deliberately watching the transcriptions from inside me /
A bouquet of tulips trailing Rose-like / clusters I have known

this book since I was young / and this sentence:
Something about this writing is traitorous

                                           to all narratives
                                           that continue to be projected upon it /

*

The first time I read from The Blood Barn /
I said it while it was unfinished

while it could be unreal / crumpled Tulip
in a dream hole *Does it require belief?*

A display and a direct address A pre document and shame /
I'm upset talking about singing myself talking about singing myself /

*

                                      N describes hearing me read it / as a
                                      novel / Listening to The Blood Barn / It
                                      felt like a novel, he says /

I touch my odd gray skirt I can't gather it It is physically impossible I am not in my original state I thought it would be an essay / but in my life I've never written prose / I described to N knowing / before I wrote poems / that I would never write poems / *What are you / writing? What are we / writing? What kind of space does it take?*

A phrase that doesn't go on *What happened to the lyric?* These questions / my body hurt A novel A woman / answering questions says, A sense of self that is already there. There's no language or mark for leaving a trace of it. Someone who is truly rooted in life isn't writing novels, a woman /asking questions says. She isn't writing novels but she is

What is this if not / hers

*

I am not in my original state, I think when I finish reading The Blood Barn.

*

////////When I am not finished writing / I am thinking

////////of how much / we hate all the forms that women take

////////We hate all the forms bodies suffer from / or make possible

////////for themselves

////////We hate everything that happens to them

////////"How much of my life is spent / reminding myself of my life,"

////////says A in writing I spend reading

////////When I am not finished writing / I am thinking

////////I will never be able to gather it / my life / poetry

////////but I will be surrounded by it

*

For the marathon, I had to wear a costume / I remember for the marathon / The Blood Barn / the pain in my hip dressed as a run on sentence / It PEELS AND PEELS / I pinned a sign to my back / I woke up early and wrote in the darkness / I pinned a sign to my back that said:

I RAN THIS MILE AND THEN I RAN ANOTHER MILE AND THEN I RAN ANOTHER MILE AND THEN I RAN ANOTHER MILE AND THEN I RAN AND I RAN AND I RAN I RAN ANOTHER MILE AND I RAN AND I RAN THIS MILE AND I RAN THIS MILE AND I WILL RUN ANOTHER MILE AND I WILL RUN AND I WILL RUN AND I RAN AND I RAN THIS MILE AND I WILL RUN ANOTHER I RUN I RUN A MILE AND THEN I RUN I RAN A MILE I RAN THIS MILE AND I WILL RUN ANOTHER AND ANOTHER AND I RUN I RUN THIS MILE I CAN RUN THIS MILE AND THEN I RUN ANOTHER AND ANOTHER I RUN AND RUN AND RUN AND RUN AND RUN.

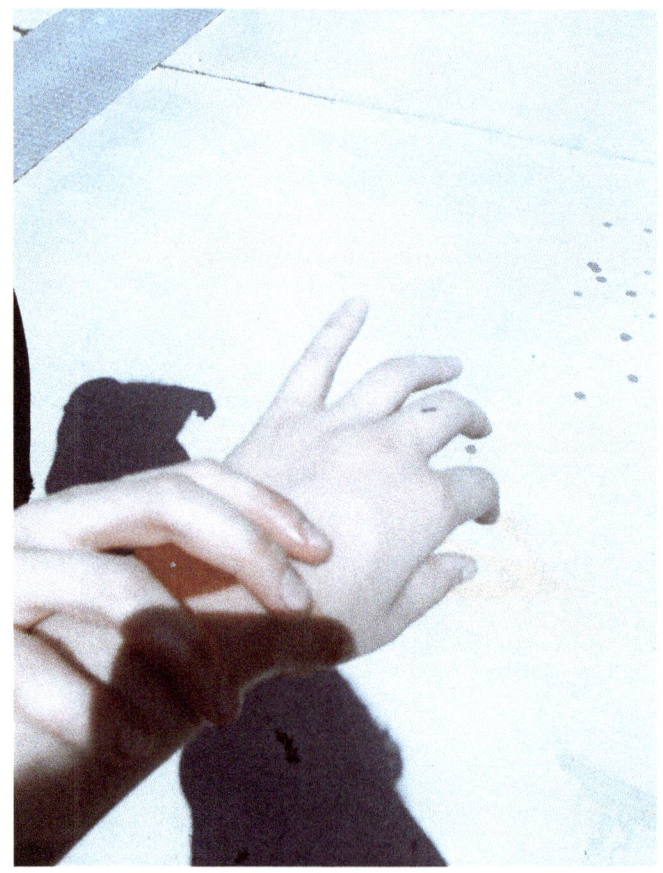

I am not in my original state ////

                                        This will never look like a poem / to you / or end

❋

I ran until my hip was nothing but scar tissue and a doctor / telling me to try eating butter / to try putting a vague feeling / or prayer at the end of this poem. My uneven body, a small curve in my spine / in my root I might never have felt except that I tried to run / to be a sentence / a word / a hard look that couldn't end / That is still here with My beautiful friend J My beautiful body was here My beautiful friend / My beautiful body Who can bear it. I remember lying on the floor next to a bowl of oatmeal I couldn't remember how to touch my body to / and a woman holding me. I have always called it The Blood Barn / The starving / ecstatic teenage girl / a student about to be 20 / An attempt that was never vain / *Would you describe her as vain? Would you still describe her painful body / as clearly pleading for your help / Is her presence such / a distraction* / I am flinching or free / the girl Flesh of carnation / Who folded in on herself so that her thinking / her pain could be exactly as private as it was public *Would you still describe her as a painful body / that didn't do anything but try / to be desirable?* / What if it was an attempt to be a force a secret moving apart / An attempt to say, No, I will not move through the world as desirable / *a body of little suns I cut a body into little suns* There was thick dark hair on my arms A violent achievement of feeling / I wanted to be alive someplace else /

When I began The Blood Barn, I wanted to write someplace else / the poem / You "writing poems, an employee" don't know how much it shows you / You don't know how much my body shows what it holds *Does it require belief?* / I want to be able to write about how this saved / my life It is inexpressible / my body's capability I am a citizen of this garden / Surprising Carnations + Fish = Book / = a haunt sort of girl.

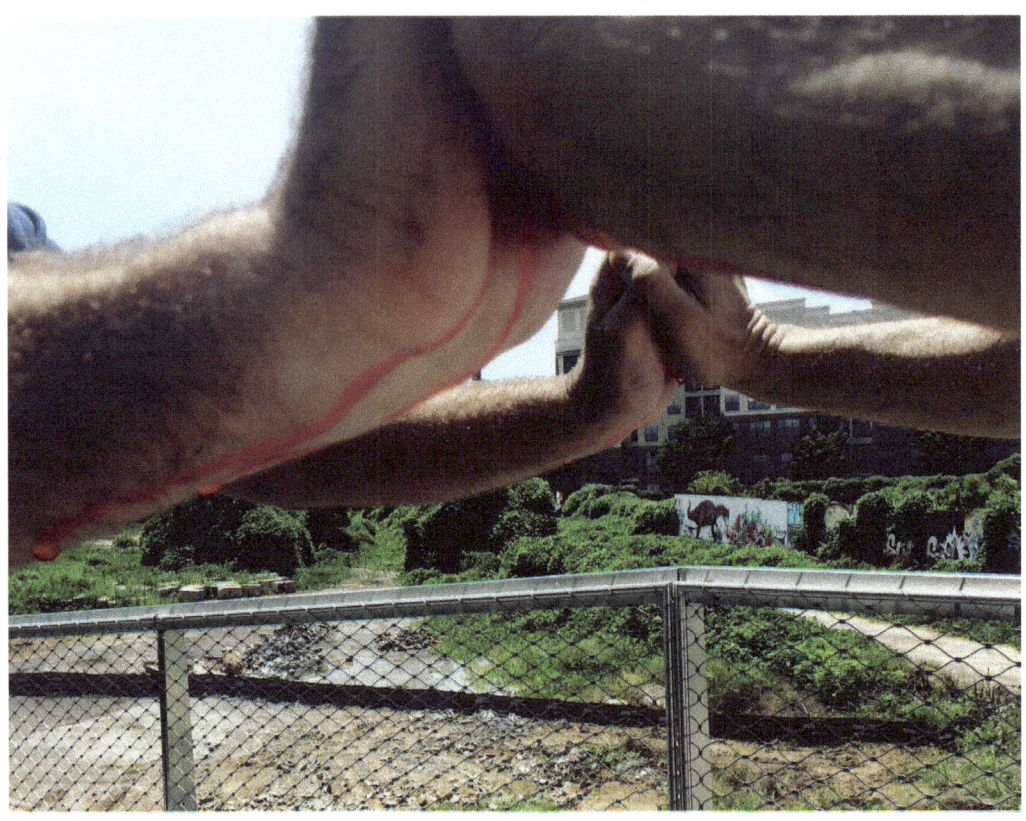

What is anorexia to the girl? When I began / The Blood Barn, I knew I was writing about how emotion / trauma / illness / every sentence has moved or does moves through this body / What it does to acknowledge what happens / to create a word / out of a phrase / out of shitting flowers / for what does go on.

※

But how it felt, / what I came to feel while writing this surprised me / It displaced me.

*

Not long after I read The Blood Barn out loud and unfinished, I read Maggie Nelson's *The Argonauts* and spent time thinking about the presence of her mother. *Who is a consequence / What is consequence* Not long after I read The Blood Barn out loud and unfinished, the tendons in my wrist swelled and suddenly hurt. *Are you still / where you were living? What kind of space does it take?*

I don't know my body but am fabulously intimate with my body. I don't know my body but I've come to see, in this writing, that recovery isn't the form I commit and commit to / that isn't going to touch what exists there / what is needed to continue / To move a hurt cardinal out of the road when before / you didn't. I don't know my body but feel angry when Maggie Nelson describes her mother / a woman who refuses to eat / and it feels like I'm supposed to think she's the weak little body / A desperation. I don't disagree I remember /

A desperation / buying diet pills + *People* magazine at CVS with a credit card / running seventy miles a week / A bitch w/ hips so tight they turn down and 2 the left in excess A bitch passing out reading *Women in Love* / A bitch rubbed raw / scrubbing the puke out of her bedroom carpet at her parents' house / after I had to pretend to eat. But is this the center / pity + a thinness / a narrative for the presumed body / that predictably succumbs / ?? / to obliteration / via maleness + heterosexual fever / ?? / to pulling her blood / her secret / her inside as close to an exposed surface as possible / ?? /

The BLOOD BARN / Carrie LORIG

What saves her / I don't know my body but am fabulously intimate with my body / I know a power / that hates bodies and I could I live in fear of seeing myself / my body but I still want to insist / None of this works for me None of this is / me, a narrative. Not long after I read The Blood Barn out loud and unfinished, I held my wrist and knew I was writing this / I held my wrist and knew I was feeling this / *What is a descendant of sensitivity?* A swell and a poem about a secret / other kindness dangerously another so I could experience her / a woman as real / I put my body against it and I move apart there / How is a citation, something you've never read, a thing you are reading / a girl.

Question: What is poetry? Why do you write it?

a)

To trace multiple accounts of the word.

To trace how the word impels or impales the body / the flower.

As things spill over.

As density is unloaded.

As rhythm is unloaded, rhythm strays.

As rhythm strays, it realigns with the tilt of the cave / of the mouth.

To repeat yourself.

To repeat someone else.

To repeat but mean something else.

To repeat what is unquotable.

To find language unquotable.

To use language anyway.

To experiment / to trace the urgency which impels or impales.

To render absence.

How to render absence.

How to be a protrusion.

To wear a headdress despite the absence / protrusion felt.

To be a pug in a headdress.

To be a cliff in a headdress.

To wrap the hair in yarn.

To wrap the hair in wound.

To wrap the hair in caves.

To wrap the hair in flowers.

To warp.

To consider violation / violence / volition / vividness.

To ask / what it is to describe.

What it means. How it means.

To be haunted by description / its possibility.

To ditch (in) the throat, to mispronounce it.

To feed.

To see it floral / love.

How to speak. How to utter.

b)

The Devil inside me / The Flower inside me

What happened to the lyric?

Have you ever felt safe in your body?

No.

❊

This isn't the story of a girl.

This is a girl who saw purple, then green, then orange, then sea foam, then navy.

crumpled Tulip in a dream hole *Does it require belief?*

❊

❋

When I began The Blood Barn, I had begun seeing a chiropractor because the pain in my hip, a pain that began during the peak of anorexia, had returned. A scar tissue, a hard dead fog.

Then, every way I was looked at and examined revealed nothing. Then, a hard dead fog rubbed me and rubbed me and soaked me doctors rubbed me and rubbed me with therapists and butter and shots of cortisol and electrical pulses soaked me until I left the country and did something like not turn away from my body / with feeling.

I have not seen my body since any of this happened, but I do feel it. A big dead fog or a ghost or my remains looking at me or a girl falling down in the snow. *What is a consequence? Who is a consequence?*

❋

It's been almost a year since I began The Blood Barn and now, the chiropractor, who has the same name as a poet, she holds my wrist / a hard dead fog doctors rubbed with braces and butter / she holds my wrist / the one I melted a red ice cube on / She holds my wrist and says, It's travelled hasn't it.

I work to not cry every time I speak with her. Not because I'm sad / but because I'm often overwhelmed at the amount of feeling we are able to exchange when we're close in proximity and attention. I can't often say what those feelings even are / what they are attached to for each of us / I don't know her I can only acknowledge it / *Am I even a poet*.

I leave work to go somewhere else / I leave work where my body is told to hold it and hold it and hold it / I leave work as the girl possessed and eating an orange / I leave work in August / having just turned 30 / the weak little body strong as life strong as violets / having never turned away from trying / to understand how this poem is changing citation / narrative / healing / a physical means for me.

Do you live in a state of repercussion?

I let a red ice cube melt on my wrist and I decide to go to a myofascial release therapist named Carl Another C / A desperation / but one meant to give language to my body / instead of to this poem / to any poem.

The man A kind of oval / An odd witness A kind body / Another C / holds my wrist / presses my sternum / presses my ears and moves it apart there / the fascia the entire spread of Her massive tissue / recombines or melts there into the weak little body's flinches / strong as life strong as violets / I come home

and lay my hand on my stomach and tell N that I will never write poems / but I will lay my hand on my stomach and for the first time / feel something there like presence / like touching / my body as it is / I come home and lay my hand on my stomach and tell N the question I need / a question put tenderly and suddenly towards / by Another C

Have you ever felt safe in your body?

The girl faces freedom and it is excruciating. I'm terrified this / the way I construct something / the activity in my body a form / is unlistenable / unreadable / I can only write here / I can only never write poems / that are poems my body here / strong as life strong as violets To move a hurt cardinal out of the road when before / you didn't.

What Spilled / In the Velvet Jungle / From Where:

<u>In the first Blood Barn</u>
-The question *"What happened to the lyric?"* and the text that follows it originally appeared as part of a post "Young Poets Bare All: What is a Culture?" and curation by Amy King at the Poetry Foundation's *Harriet* blog on August 28, 2015.

<u>In the second Blood Barn</u>
-paperwork from Dr. Amy King's office appears.

-Mark Cugini sent me a text.

<u>In the third Blood Barn</u>
-The portion of this poem which is a Letter to C (Carrie) from L (Leora) was written by Leora Fridman and originally published on VIDA's website on September 29, 2015 with the title, "Reports from the Field: Letter to C." This whole poem is dedicated to her.

-Photos of Pluto came from New Horizons, NASA's mission to the Pluto system and Kuiper Belt.

-The Ace of Cups / is from the Emily Dickinson Tarot Deck, which is sold by Factory Hollow Press. The cups suit was designed by Haley Rene Thompson.

-"IT'S GONNA BITE YR FEELINGS OUT" and "I COULD LEAVE THE PARTY WITHOUT EVER LETTING YOU KNOW" are lyrics from Kiiara's "Gold."

-My work always owes a great deal to Bhanu Kapil. Bhanu Kapil's blog can be found here: http://jackkerouacispunjabi.blogspot.com/

-Re-imaginations / versions of a question Kapil has been asking (Who are we when we are not with each other?) appear in this poem.

-Thank you Brandon Shimoda for sending me *Evening Oracle* (Letter Machine Editions) and for the postcard.

-Thank you Audrey Patterson / all the students at the Art Academy of Cincinnati.

-The photo of the girl in an orange hat is me. I am in college and I am 19 or 20.

-Leora Fridman sent me a text on New Year's Day. A still from a video I sent her via text on New Year's Day also appears.

-We were both wrong / We listened to the recording. Alice Notley doesn't say break the song. She actually says destroy the song.

<u>In the fourth Blood Barn</u>
-All molecules / the blood that comes out of my face in the night / are left-handed: http://www.radiolab.org/story/122613-mirror-mirror/

-The photo of my mother was taken and developed by father, Bob Lorig, who is a photographer.

-Listen to Joanna Newsom's "Pin-Light Bent."

In the fifth Blood Barn
-What precedes this poem / Surprising Carnations + Fish = Book / was written by my dearest J, Jared Joseph.

-"If we're going to heal / let it be glorious" and "1,000 girls raise their arms" appear in Beyoncé's *Lemonade*.

-"Yes, I deserve a spring—I owe nobody nothing" comes from Virginia Woolf's *A Writer's Diary*.

-Thank you to Brandon Shimoda. Thank you for asking me questions after reading *The Book of Repulsive Women*.

-To create the page that says PEEL, I took a photograph of one of the pages in Jean-Michel Basquiat's journals and traced, in red, what had first been written in black. Basquiat's journals were on display as part of an exhibit called, "Basquiat: The Unknown Notebooks," at the High Museum of Art Atlanta.

-The photo from Instagram is of Anna Betbeze's "Nine Planets in the Dark House" (2015), which was at the High Museum of Art Atlanta.

-Reading Aimé Césaire and Etel Adnan helped me reach "I cut a body into little suns."

-"few women ever experience themselves as real" was inspired by Andrea Dworkin's *Our Blood: Prophecies and Discourses on Sexual Politics*. Elanor

McInerney is the reason I read it.

-A line from Anne Sexton's "The Truth the Dead Know" appears.

-Reading Alice Notley's "Songs for the Second Unborn Baby," and the poem, "30th Birthday," helped me complete this poem.

-Thank you Ginger Ko + Raquel Salas-Rivera for being the reason I was able to first read one of The Blood Barns out loud. Thank you for your poems.

-Photos of my (injured) wrist and other hands w/ red ice cubes comes from a workshop I led through Lost in the Letters on my 30th birthday. Thank you Stephanie Dowda + Scott Daughtridge.

-Bodies, I love you. Thank you Amy + Carl + Nick for helping mine.

Acknowledgments:

"The Blood Barn" (1) and "The Blood Barn" (2) were published in *The Pinch Journal*.

"The Blood Barn" (3) was published in *DREGINALD*.

"The Blood Barn" (4) was published in *FANZINE*.

"The Blood Barn" (5) was published in *The Brooklyn Rail*.

www.ingramcontent.com/pod-product-compliance
Lightning Source LLC
Chambersburg PA
CBHW061149070526
44584CB00034B/4469